DISORDER IN THE AMERICAN COURTS

Actual quotes, word for word,
from real court proceedings!

Presented by CourtComics.com

EDITED AND COMPILED BY MARCELLE BOREN

ILLUSTRATED BY SONNY SCHUG

If a wise man goes to court with a foolish man,
the fool rages or scoffs, and there is no peace.
Proverbs 29:9

Published by Iwahu Publishing
iwahupublishing@gmail.com

ISBN-13:978-0692676646
ISBN-10:0692676643

The following quotes are things people actually said, word for word, under oath in legal court proceedings. Some proper names and place names have been changed to protect the guilty until proven innocent. And, of course, punctuation is merely a suggestion, right?

CONTENTS

PART 1: ANIMALS

1

2

3

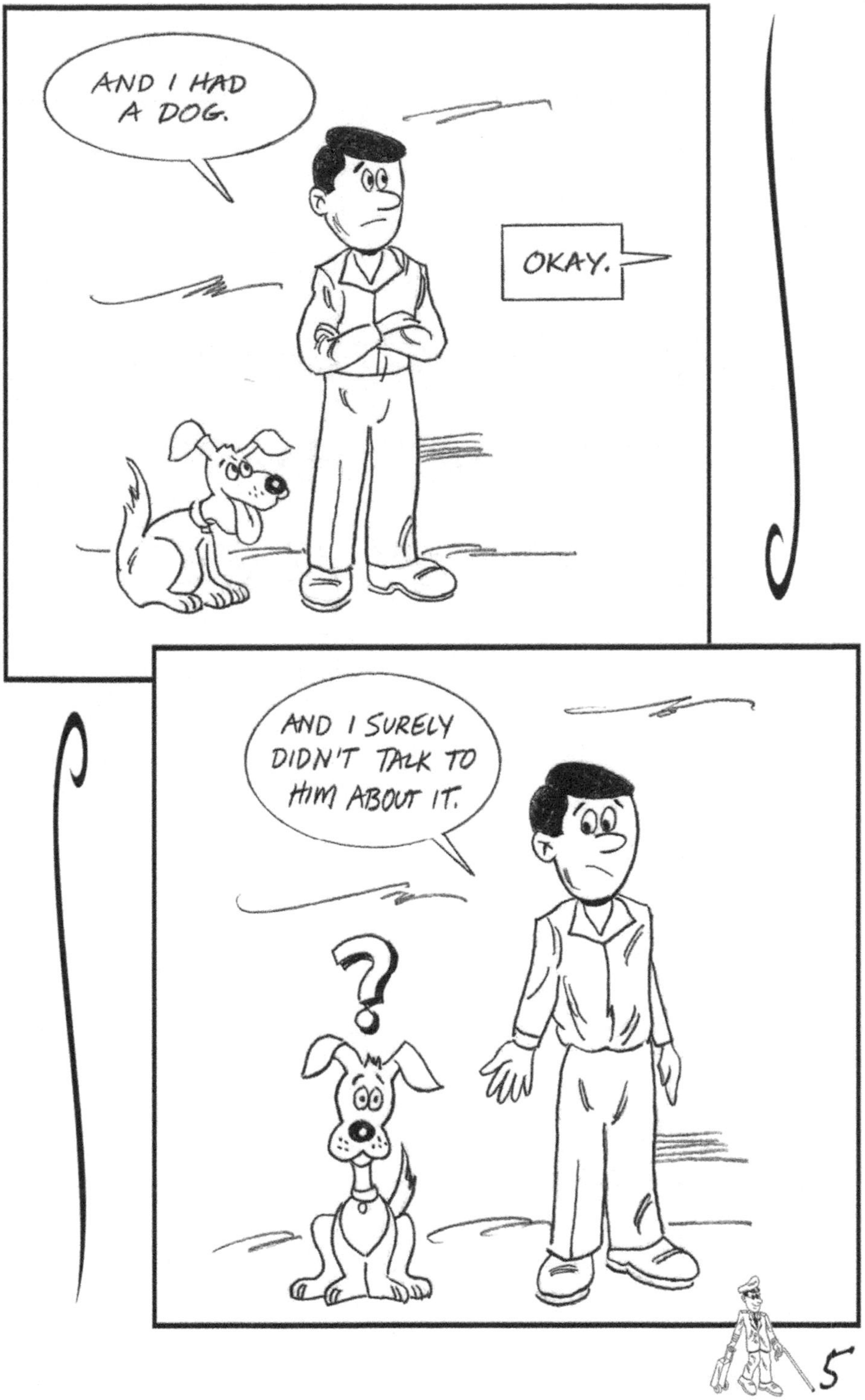
AND I HAD A DOG.
OKAY.
AND I SURELY DIDN'T TALK TO HIM ABOUT IT.
?

PART 2: PLANES, TRAINS AND AUTOMOBILES

7

PART 3: ANATOMY AND PHYSIOLOGY

12

13

14

15

MY MOTHER KEPT UP WITH ALL OF HER SUPPLIES THAT SHE NEEDED FOR HER UROSTOMY AND HER COLOSTOMY BAG. AND SHE WAS VERY ANAL ABOUT GETTING HER STUFF.

WHEN YOU TWISTED YOUR ANKLE, WHERE DID YOU HAVE THE SENSATION OF ANY PAIN?
IN THE ANKLE.

17

PART 4: ACCIDENTS

20

22

23

PART 5: ALL IN A DAY'S WORK

28

29

30

PART 6: Q and A

35

36

37

38

40

41

42

PART 7: MEMORY

45

I WORK ALL—
I REALLY—TAKES ME ALL DAY TO CLEAN MY HOUSE, BUT I THINK IT'S BECAUSE I FORGET WHAT I'M DOING, YOU KNOW?
FIDO

TELL ME EVERYTHING YOU CAN RECALL ABOUT THAT CONVERSATION.
WELL, I CAN TELL YOU IT WAS NIGHTIME.
I DON'T KNOW WHAT TIME OF DAY.

48

PART 8: MONEY
MATTERS

51

52

53

54

PART 9: PLANNING AND PAPERWORK

57

60

PART 10: MARRIAGE

63

65

66

67

68

PART II: KNOWLEDGE IS POWER

I CAN'T DISPUTE THAT. WHOEVER SAID THAT WAS RIGHT.
THAT WAS ME. THAT'S CORRECT.

73

74

75

76

PART 12: STATING THE OBVIOUS

78

79

80

BUT FOR WHAT PURPOSE DID YOU BELIEVE THAT YOU NEEDED TO HAVE THESE FOUR WATER FILTRATION DEVICES FOR YOUR STORE?
FOR THE WATER.

HOW WOULD YOU DESCRIBE THE AMOUNT OF WATER THAT GOT INTO THE DINING ROOM?
WET.

PART 13: WHAT?

83

PART 14: ATTORNEYS, CLIENTS AND LAWSUITS

88

I DON'T KNOW IF I'M REALLY SUPPOSED TO SAY WHAT I'M THINKING.
OH, YEAH, YOU ARE. JUST LET IT HANG OUT. IT'S A LAWSUIT. IT'S OKAY.

THIS IS A FORMAL PROCEEDING, BUT IT DOESN'T HAVE TO BE A JERK PROCEEDING; OKAY?

91

92

93

PART 15: CORRESPONDENCE

BUT I THINK EVERYONE IN THE WORLD, GENERALLY, WHO GETS MAIL AND WANTS TO KNOW WHAT IT SAYS SHOULD OPEN IT UP AND SHOULD LOOK AT IT.

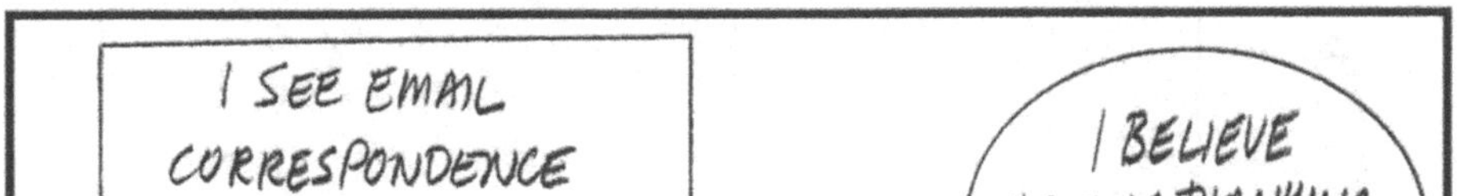
I SEE EMAIL CORRESPONDENCE BETWEEN YOU AND JIM. AND IT SAYS, "THANKS FOR YOUR HELP." WHAT WAS THIS ABOUT?
I BELIEVE HE WAS THANKING ME FOR MY HELP.

96

97

PART 16: TO YOUR HEALTH

102

PART 17: LET'S NOT MINCE WORDS

THEY SAID, "'DIVISION' IS DIVISIVE. DON'T USE IT."

OKAY.

SO OLD PEOPLE LIKE ME IGNORED THEM, AND YOUNG PEOPLE DON'T NOTICE.

107

ALL IS AN ALL-ENCOMPASSING WORD.
ALL

IS THAT YES?
THAT IS YES. YES, IT IS. THAT IS YES.
YES

110

PART 18: AIRHEADS

112

113

114

115

116

STOP
DO NOT ENTER
LIKE I SAY, I CAN'T ENTER HIS PERSONAL LIFE BECAUSE I AM NOT PERSONALLY HIM.

I'LL TRY NOT TO CONFUSE ME.

118

PART 19: LIFE AND DEATH

123

PART 20: FRIENDS AND FAMILY

125

126

128

129

PART 21:
HODGEPODGE

132

133

135

137

138